KING ARTHUR

It is the year 650, and the people of England are not happy. There is no king and there is a lot of fighting. One night, Merlin the magician has a dream. 'I see a wonderful king. His name is Arthur!'

Merlin finds Arthur – he is young, but he learns fast. Soon he is a strong, good king, and the people of England are happy again. Then Arthur meets a beautiful woman, Guinevere. 'I want to marry Guinevere,' Arthur tells Merlin. But Merlin is not happy. 'I see a dark future for you and Guinevere,' he says.

Can Arthur and Guinevere be happy? What is this dark future? And who are Arthur's true friends?

OXFORD BOOKWORMS LIBRARY
Human Interest

King Arthur

Starter (250 headwords)

RETOLD BY JANET HARDY-GOULD

King Arthur

Illustrated by
Axel Rator

OXFORD UNIVERSITY PRESS

OXFORD
UNIVERSITY PRESS

Great Clarendon Street, Oxford OX2 6DP

Oxford University Press is a department of the University of Oxford.
It furthers the University's objective of excellence in research, scholarship,
and education by publishing worldwide in

Oxford New York

Auckland Cape Town Dar es Salaam Hong Kong Karachi
Kuala Lumpur Madrid Melbourne Mexico City Nairobi
New Delhi Shanghai Taipei Toronto

With offices in

Argentina Austria Brazil Chile Czech Republic France Greece
Guatemala Hungary Italy Japan Poland Portugal Singapore
South Korea Switzerland Thailand Turkey Ukraine Vietnam

OXFORD and OXFORD ENGLISH are registered trade marks of
Oxford University Press in the UK and in certain other countries

ISBN: 978 0 19 423414 6

Printed in China

Word count (main text): 1140

For more information on the Oxford Bookworms Library, visit
www.oup.com/elt/gradedreaders

This book is printed on paper from certified and well-managed sources.

CONTENTS

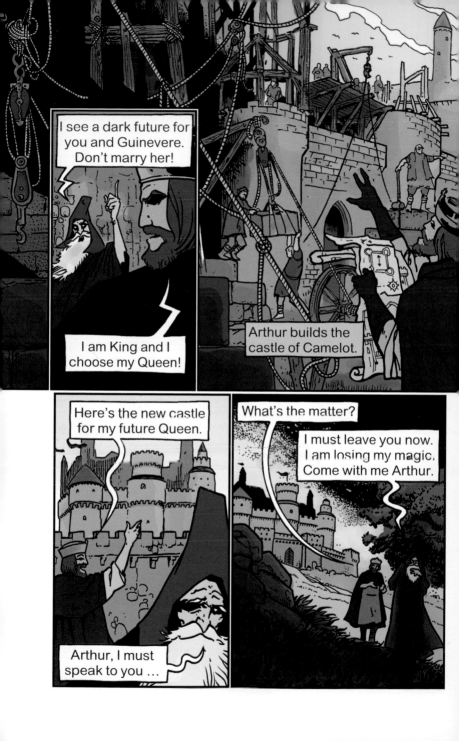

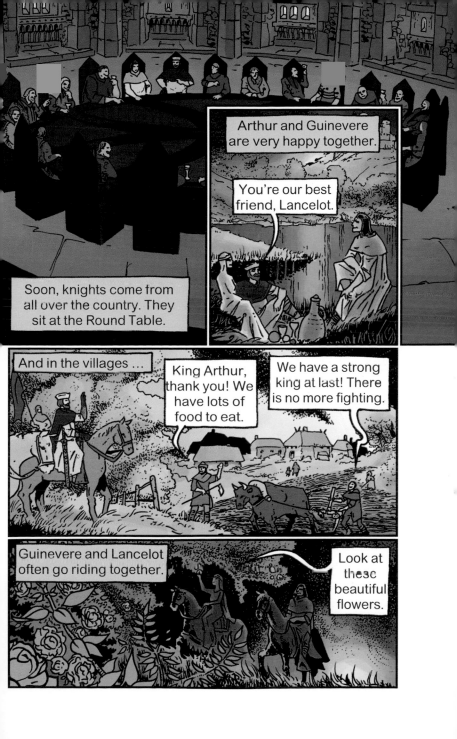

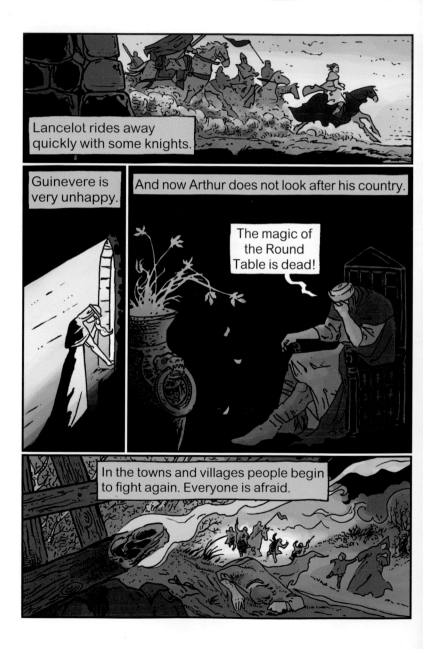

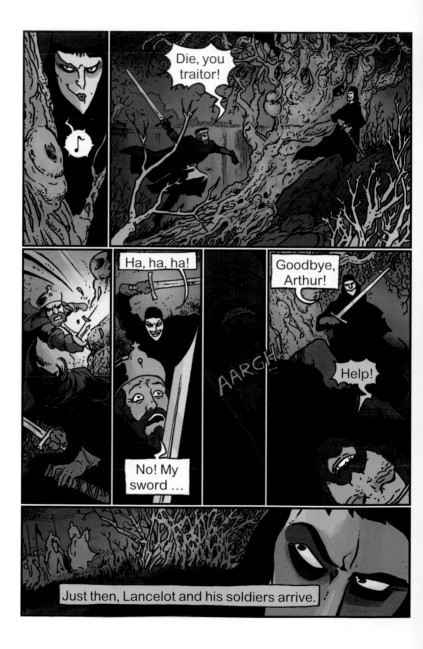

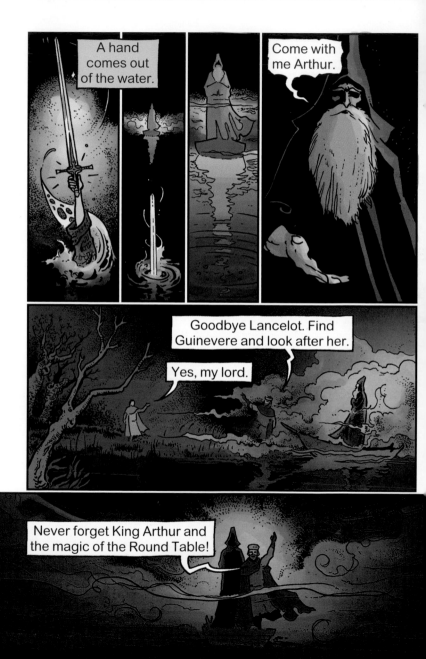

GLOSSARY

beat win a fight against a person
break make something go into smaller pieces
choose take the thing or person that you like the best
competition a game that people try to win
crown a special thing that a king wears on his head
dream pictures inside your head when you sleep
future *(adj)* of the time that happens sometime after today
future *(n)* the time that happens sometime after today
king the most important man in the country
knight a soldier with a horse, in the time of King Arthur
look after take care of somebody
lord a very important man with a lot of land and money
magic *(n)* a special power that can make wonderful or
    strange things happen
magician somebody who makes strange things happen
marry take somebody as your husband or wife
the North the direction on your left when you watch the
    sun come up in the morning
prison a place where bad people are locked up
pull move something strongly towards you
queen the wife of a king
soldier a person in an army
strong *(adj)* having a powerful body
throw lift something up and send it quickly through the air
traitor someone who goes against his king or his country
try see if you can do something
win be the best in a game

King Arthur

ACTIVITIES

ACTIVITIES

Before Reading

1 **Look at the picture on the cover of the book. Now answer these questions.**

1 Where do you think the story happens?

a ☐ Japan.

b ☐ England.

c ☐ Spain.

d ☐ Australia.

2 When do you think the story happens?

a ☐ Ten years ago.

b ☐ Fifty years ago.

c ☐ A hundred years ago.

d ☐ Over a thousand years ago.

2 **Read the back cover of the book. Which of these words do you think are in the story? Put a tick next to them. Perhaps not all of them are in the story. Why not?**

horse	soldier	gun
car	pop star	castle
bicycle	queen	supermarket
ride	marry	America
drive	sword	village

ACTIVITIES

While Reading

1 **Read pages 1–4, then answer these questions.**

Who . . .
1 puts the sword in the stone? Why?
2 pulls the sword out of the stone?
3 is Arthur's half-sister? What can she do?
4 wins the battle?

2 **Read pages 5–7.**
Are these sentences true (T) or false (F)?

	T	F
1 Arthur and Guinevere talk for a long time.	☐	☐
2 Merlin wants Arthur to marry Guinevere.	☐	☐
3 Merlin builds a new castle.	☐	☐
4 Merlin shows Arthur a magic sword.	☐	☐

3 **Read pages 8–11. Now answer these questions.**

1 What does Guinevere give Arthur?
2 Who fights a lot of different men?
3 Who is the strongest knight in England?
4 Why are the people in the villages happy?

4 Read pages 12–15. Who says these words?

1 'You must be king, my son.'

2 'Be careful, Arthur. Mordred is a bad man.'

3 'Oh Lancelot. You're very strong!'

4 'Perhaps Guinevere and Lancelot are in love.'

5 'Leave Camelot now, before I kill you.'

5 Read pages 16–20.
Are these sentences true (T) or false (F)?

	T	F
1 Guinevere is happy because Lancelot leaves Camelot.	☐	☐
2 In the villages the people start to fight.	☐	☐
3 Arthur fights a battle against Lancelot.	☐	☐
4 Mordred puts Guinevere in prison.	☐	☐
5 Arthur wants to fight Mordred on the next day.	☐	☐

6 Before you read pages 21–24,
can you guess what happens?

	YES	NO
1 Arthur breaks his magic sword.	☐	☐
2 Arthur kills Mordred.	☐	☐
3 Mordred kills Arthur.	☐	☐
4 Lancelot arrives and kills Mordred.	☐	☐
5 Arthur is king of England again.	☐	☐
6 Arthur dies and Merlin takes him away.	☐	☐
7 Guinevere marries Lancelot.	☐	☐

ACTIVITIES

After Reading

1 **Put these nine sentences in the right order.**

a ☐ Lancelot leaves Camelot.

b ☐ Lancelot is the first knight of the Round Table.

c ☐ Arthur pulls the sword out of the stone.

d ☐ Arthur wants to fight a battle against Lancelot.

e ☐ Merlin makes a magic stone and puts a sword in it.

f ☐ Mordred hits Arthur with a sword.

g ☐ Morgan and Mordred arrive one night at Camelot.

h ☐ Arthur leaves in a boat with Merlin.

i ☐ Arthur marries Guinevere.

2 **Who says this? Who do they say it to?**

1 'Don't be afraid! With my help you can be king.' .... says this to ....

2 'Shall I fight in your name?' .... says this to ....

3 'Guinevere and Lancelot are often together.' .... says this to ....

4 'No ... no ... not today. Let's fight tomorrow.' .... says this to ....

5 'Find Guinevere and look after her.' .... says this to ....

3 Look at each picture, then answer the questions after it.

1 Who is this?
What is he doing?

2 What is this?
Who builds it?

3 Who is this?

4 Who is this?

5 Who is this?
Why is she crying?

6 Who are these people?
What happens next?

7 Who is this?   What happens next?

ABOUT THE AUTHOR

Janet Hardy-Gould is an experienced teacher and teacher trainer. She lives in Brighton, on the south coast of England, with her husband Geoff and two children, Gabriella and Joseph. She is interested in European history and wrote about Henry the Eighth, an important English King, in *Henry VIII and his Six Wives* (Stage 2, True Stories) for the Oxford Bookworms Library.

OXFORD BOOKWORMS LIBRARY

Classics • Crime & Mystery • Factfiles • Fantasy & Horror
Human Interest • Playscripts • Thriller & Adventure
True Stories • World Stories

The OXFORD BOOKWORMS LIBRARY provides enjoyable reading in English, with a wide range of classic and modern fiction, non-fiction, and plays. It includes original and adapted texts in seven carefully graded language stages, which take learners from beginner to advanced level. An overview is given on the next pages.

All Stage 1 titles are available as audio recordings, as well as over eighty other titles from Starter to Stage 6. All Starters and many titles at Stages 1 to 4 are specially recommended for younger learners. Every Bookworm is illustrated, and Starters and Factfiles have full-colour illustrations.

The OXFORD BOOKWORMS LIBRARY also offers extensive support. Each book contains an introduction to the story, notes about the author, a glossary, and activities. Additional resources include tests and worksheets, and answers for these and for the activities in the books. There is advice on running a class library, using audio recordings, and the many ways of using Oxford Bookworms in reading programmes. Resource materials are available on the website <www.oup.com/elt/gradedreaders>.

The *Oxford Bookworms Collection* is a series for advanced learners. It consists of volumes of short stories by well-known authors, both classic and modern. Texts are not abridged or adapted in any way, but carefully selected to be accessible to the advanced student.

You can find details and a full list of titles in the *Oxford Bookworms Library Catalogue* and *Oxford English Language Teaching Catalogues*, and on the website <www.oup.com/elt/gradedreaders>.

THE OXFORD BOOKWORMS LIBRARY
GRADING AND SAMPLE EXTRACTS

STARTER • 250 HEADWORDS

present simple – present continuous – imperative –
can/cannot, must – *going to* (future) – simple gerunds …

Her phone is ringing – but where is it?

Sally gets out of bed and looks in her bag. No phone. She looks under the bed. No phone. Then she looks behind the door. There is her phone. Sally picks up her phone and answers it. *Sally's Phone*

STAGE 1 • 400 HEADWORDS

… past simple – coordination with *and, but, or* –
subordination with *before, after, when, because, so* …

I knew him in Persia. He was a famous builder and I worked with him there. For a time I was his friend, but not for long. When he came to Paris, I came after him – I wanted to watch him. He was a very clever, very dangerous man. *The Phantom of the Opera*

STAGE 2 • 700 HEADWORDS

… present perfect – *will* (future) – *(don't) have to, must not, could* –
comparison of adjectives – simple *if* clauses – past continuous –
tag questions – *ask/tell* + infinitive …

While I was writing these words in my diary, I decided what to do. I must try to escape. I shall try to get down the wall outside. The window is high above the ground, but I have to try. I shall take some of the gold with me – if I escape, perhaps it will be helpful later. *Dracula*

STAGE 3 • 1000 HEADWORDS

... should, may – present perfect continuous – *used to* – past perfect –
causative – relative clauses – indirect statements ...

Of course, it was most important that no one should see
Colin, Mary, or Dickon entering the secret garden. So Colin
gave orders to the gardeners that they must all keep away
from that part of the garden in future. ***The Secret Garden***

STAGE 4 • 1400 HEADWORDS

... past perfect continuous – passive (simple forms) –
would conditional clauses – indirect questions –
relatives with *where/when* – gerunds after prepositions/phrases ...

I was glad. Now Hyde could not show his face to the world
again. If he did, every honest man in London would be proud
to report him to the police. ***Dr Jekyll and Mr Hyde***

STAGE 5 • 1800 HEADWORDS

... future continuous – future perfect –
passive (modals, continuous forms) –
would have conditional clauses – modals + perfect infinitive ...

If he had spoken Estella's name, I would have hit him. I was so
angry with him, and so depressed about my future, that I could
not eat the breakfast. Instead I went straight to the old house.
Great Expectations

STAGE 6 • 2500 HEADWORDS

... passive (infinitives, gerunds) – advanced modal meanings –
clauses of concession, condition

When I stepped up to the piano, I was confident. It was as if I
knew that the prodigy side of me really did exist. And when I
started to play, I was so caught up in how lovely I looked that
I didn't worry how I would sound. ***The Joy Luck Club***

BOOKWORMS · HUMAN INTEREST · STARTER

Robin Hood

JOHN ESCOTT

'You're a brave man, but I am afraid for you,' says Lady Marian to Robin of Locksley. She is afraid because Robin does not like Prince John's new taxes and wants to do something for the poor people of Nottingham. When Prince John hears this, Robin is suddenly in danger – great danger.

BOOKWORMS · HUMAN INTEREST · STARTER

Star Reporter

JOHN ESCOTT

'There's a new girl in town,' says Joe, and soon Steve is out looking for her. Marietta is easy to find in a small town, but every time he sees her something goes wrong . . . and his day goes from bad to worse.

BOOKWORMS · THRILLER & ADVENTURE · STARTER

The White Stones

LESTER VAUGHAN

'The people on this island don't like archaeologists,' the woman on the ferry says. You only want to study the 4,500 year-old Irish megalithic stones but very soon strange things begin to happen to you. Can you solve the mystery in time?

BOOKWORMS · CRIME & MYSTERY · STARTER

Mystery in London

HELEN BROOKE

Six women are dead because of the Whitechapel Killer. Now another woman lies in a London street and there is blood everywhere. She is very ill. You are the famous detective Mycroft Pound; can you catch the killer before he escapes?

BOOKWORMS · FANTASY & HORROR · STAGE 1

Aladdin and the Enchanted Lamp

RETOLD BY JUDITH DEAN

In a city in Arabia there lives a boy called Aladdin. He is poor and often hungry, but one day he finds an old lamp. When he rubs the lamp, smoke comes out of it, and then out of the smoke comes a magical jinnee.

With the jinnee's help, Aladdin is soon rich, with gold and jewels and many fine things. But can he win the love of the Sultan's daughter, the beautiful Princess Badr-al-Budur?

BOOKWORMS · TRUE STORIES · STAGE 1

Henry VIII and his Six Wives

JANET HARDY-GOULD

There were six of them – three Katherines, two Annes, and a Jane. One of them was the King's wife for twenty-four years, another for only a year and a half. One died, two were divorced, and two were beheaded. It was a dangerous, uncertain life.

After the King's death in 1547, his sixth wife finds a box of old letters – one from each of the first five wives. They are sad, angry, frightened letters. They tell the story of what it was like to be the wife of Henry VIII of England.